YOU ARE ACCEPTED

In Conversation with Paul Tillich

~ A Poetic Discourse: On Grace After the Fall ~

SAINT JULIAN PRESS

Praise for *You Are Accepted*

These are poems of mature spirituality, an inner life that finds its covenant "etched not in tablets but in tears." This seasoned author uses scripture not as a destination, but as a door, opening to the radiant, yet paradoxical, dark realities of Being. More than an homage to Paul Tillich, these poems dialog with silence itself, with the heart's hollow, where, in the Psalmist's words, "depth cries unto depth." They are poems vibrant with compassion for "the poor, whose hunger teaches them to pray"; poems helping us clarify our faith. For deep faith thrives on the ineffable, on the liminal, on a "silence draped in the wreckage of our certainty." Seeds of contemplative prayer, planted in the heart, these poems thrive in a climate with John of the Cross, Julian of Norwich, and Thomas Merton. Their savor deepens with time. Return to them often. Taste them in bittersweet communion sips, like wine.

—Fred LaMotte
Strangers & Pilgrims
The Nectar of this Breath

Long known as a poet of depth, contemplative spaciousness, and ecstatic wonder, Ron Starbuck now turns his gift for interfaith dialogue towards conversation with Paul Tillich's *The Shaking of the Foundations*. In *You Are Accepted*, one has the impression of a soul moved from deep receptivity into a heightened state of consciousness and spilled onto the page as poetry. Moving always towards what is unshakable, these poems acknowledge the difficulties, uncertainties, and imperfections of being human, holding the reader in this vulnerability—known, loved, and encouraged. As Starbuck says, in language that is consistently accessible and generous, "Be still. / Be ready. / You are not alone. / You are not abandoned. / You are being made new."

—Melissa Studdard
Siddhartha, She: A Ritual Music Drama in Seven Tableaux
Dear Selection Committee
I Ate the Cosmos for Breakfast

YOU ARE ACCEPTED

~ In Conversation with Paul Tillich ~

A Poetic Discourse:
On Grace After the Fall

Ron Starbuck

SAINT JULIAN PRESS
HOUSTON

Published by
SAINT JULIAN PRESS, Inc.
2053 Cortlandt, Suite 200
Houston, Texas 77008
www.saintjulianpress.org

Print ISBN-13: 978-1-955194-47-1
eBook ISBN-13: 978-1-955194-48-8
Library of Congress Control Number: 2025940201

Cover Image: *Chiesa di San Francesco a Pienza II*
Photo by Ron Starbuck from Pienza, Italy

CONTENTS

A Wave of Light

In the Beginning Was the Word... and It Was Spoken Aloud

As a young boy, I would watch and listen as my father—pastor of a youthful United Methodist Church—rehearsed his homilies and sermons aloud, filling our home like a sanctuary. Early in the week, he composed them like symphonies on an old *Underwood typewriter* in his study. Then came the pacing—slow loops through his study, through the living room—as he read each line aloud. He memorized them until their rhythm felt like breath—until it flowed like poetry. By Sunday morning, the family had nearly memorized them as well.

Even though he devoted time to composing each sermon, he never read or preached directly from a manuscript. Instead, he memorized the entire text; his voice served as his manuscript. In his voice, I first heard the thoughts and literary expression of the theologian **Paul Tillich**.

I was nine or ten, maybe younger. I didn't know then what I was hearing—existential theology, the crisis of modern faith, the deep questions of God and being. I only knew that when my father quoted Tillich, something in his tone shifted. It grew still. Weightier. As though the words he spoke weren't just his own, but something given. Something carried.

Many years passed before I came to understand the weight of those words. Like most of us, I had to leave them for a while before returning. When I did—older, wearier, and perhaps a little wiser—what emerged was a poem. It arrived almost unbidden, as some things do when the soul is ready. It came from that single, seismic phrase Tillich gave the world:

"*Sometimes at that moment a wave of light breaks into our darkness, and it is as though a voice were saying: 'You are accepted. You are accepted, accepted by that which is greater than you...'*"

That poem became the threshold of all that follows.

What Follows

This collection of poems was written in conversation with Tillich's *The Shaking of the Foundations*, one of his most enduring works of pastoral theology and existential preaching. Each poem pairs with a chapter from that book—not as a commentary, but as a kind of liturgical echo. Where Tillich speaks with prophetic clarity, these poems listen with poetic openness. They are meditations, responses, and sometimes, whispered prayers.

You'll find familiar themes here: the courage to be, the yoke of religion, the mystery of time, the experience of the holy. But the language of poetry is different. It does not argue or persuade. It invites. It gestures toward mystery and leaves space for silence. It dares to ask questions that may never be answered—and trusts that even in the asking, there is grace.

Why This Still Matters

Tillich wrote during a time of deep crisis—haunted by world wars, disillusioned by modernity, unsure whether God could still be heard amid the ruins. That world has not disappeared. It has only changed costumes.

In our 21st century, we too live in a time of great shaking: of institutions, of identities, of inherited beliefs. The foundations we once trusted—whether cultural, religious, or personal—no longer feel as certain as they once did. And yet, Tillich bears witness: **there is something that remains unshaken**. Something that calls. Something that holds.

These poems seek that something.

They reach for the *God beyond God*—the *God above God*—the ground of being beyond all human language and concepts. The One—the Presence—who meets us not in the calm, but in the chaos; not in our clarity, but in our questions. They are written for those who are undone and being remade. For those who wait in silence. For those who pray without knowing exactly to whom. For those who dare to hope that presence is real, even when it goes unnamed.

If you are reading this now, I hope you find a voice in these pages that speaks quietly but clearly to your own life. Not to your certainty, but to your spirit.

Because sometimes—if only for a moment—
a wave of light does break in.
And a voice says:

You are accepted.

— *Ron Starbuck*
Saint Julian Press
Houston, Texas
June 2025

For Humanity

To every soul that has trembled
at the weight of existence and still dared to ask
if love might still be real—
This work is offered in thanksgiving
to Paul Tillich, who spoke of grace
as something that finds us in the ruins,
who called us back from the edge
without asking us to be better first,
only to be human.

"You are accepted."
—Paul Tillich

YOU ARE ACCEPTED

In Conversation with Paul Tillich

~ A Poetic Discourse: On Grace After the Fall ~

"...And that, that's why I wake each morning like a boy—even now, ever now! I swear to you, I could love the world again! It's the knowing all? To know, and even happily, that we meet unblessed; not in some garden of wax fruit and painted trees, that lie of Eden, but after, after the Fall, after many, many deaths. Is the knowing all? And the wish to kill is never killed, but with some gift of courage one may look into its face when it appears, and with a stroke of love---as to an idiot in the house—forgive it; again and again...forever?"

— Arthur Miller, *After the Fall (1964)*

WE ARE HELD
*After Paul Tillich's Book – **The Shaking of the Foundations***

> *"Though the earth should change, though the mountains shake in the heart of the sea... Be still, and know that I am God." — Psalm 46:2–3, 10 (NRSVA)*

Soon, without warning, comes a time
When the ground beneath us trembles,
When the structures we've trusted
Begin to crumble and fall.

In that moment of uncertainty,
When fear grips our heart,
Remember this truth:
We are held in wholeness.

Not by the shifting strands of circumstance,
But by the eternal foundation
That no earthquake can shake.

When the lights dim and shadows grow,
When the path ahead is obscured,
Even here, presence abides.
The unseen hand of grace—
The holiness binding creation—
Still supports us.

Do not despair when the familiar fades,
For in the void, new possibilities arise.
From the ruins of what was,
A new beginning dares to rise.

We are held
By the One who is unchanging,
By the love that endures all things,
By the hope that does not disappoint.

So stand firm, even as the earth quakes.
Trust in the deeper ground
Beneath all you believe and know.
We are held.

WHEN FOUNDATIONS BREAK
After Chapter 1 – "The Shaking of the Foundations"

> *For the mountains may depart and the hills be removed, but my*
> *steadfast love shall not depart from you, and my covenant of peace*
> *shall not be removed, says the Lord, who has compassion on you.*
> *— Isaiah 54:10 (NRSVA)*

We have felt the trembling—
the ground give way beneath our certainties,
the sky fracture like a mirror
unable to hold the weight of our illusions.

What once steadied us—
stone, light, word—
now slips like sand
through the fingers of time.

We have watched cities bombed
and burn down to their names,
watched children become ash
before they could speak the word: peace.
We thought these were metaphors,
but the scroll has been opened.

We are not as we were.
The world is not as it was.
Split.
Shattered.
Unmoored from meaning.

We crowned ourselves with the dust of Eden
and said: We will not die.
But we are dying.

The promises of progress, peace, prosperity—
mirages now,
flickering in the heat
of a species unwilling to turn
until the foundations give way
beneath its own brilliance.

Still—
beneath the breaking,
beneath the smoke and silence,
beneath the shaking of every structure we trusted—
there is something that does not move.

A Rock not made with hands.
A Voice still burning in the bush.
A Covenant etched not in tablets,
but in tears.

We are not without witness.

Even now,
in the wreckage,
mercy waits.

Even now,
in the ruins,
the unshakable remains.

BETWEEN THE TWO ORDERS
After Chapter 2 – "We Live in Two Orders"

> *"All people are grass, their constancy is like the flower of the field. The grass withers, the flower fades, but the word of our God will stand forever. — Isaiah 40:6–8 (NRSVA)"*

The grass withers—
and so do we.
Even the proudest bloom fades,
petal by petal,
beneath the breath of time.

We are born into exile
without a map—
only a voice in the wilderness
crying: Prepare.

But what road can be made
through the ruins of forgetting?
What comfort remains
when even strength
proves fleeting?

We are the ones who faint.
We are the ones who fall.
We are the builders of empires
now burning in their sleep.

We are those who sang of progress,
believing ourselves gods,
and woke to our undoing.

Still—
the prophet dares to speak.
Still—
the Word dares to stand.

Comfort, O comfort my people—
not because the earth has changed,
but because God has not.

We live in two orders:
one that burns,
and one that blesses.
One that fails,
and one that forgives.
One that fades like breath,
and one that breathes forever.

We have seen the nations weigh
less than dust
on the scales of eternity.

We have bowed before our idols—
fashioned from fear,
gilded with our hopes—
and still they could not hold us.

But we have also heard
the sound of wings,
rising where we thought all was fallen.

We have seen the suffering
leave a deeper mark
than the sword.

And so we say again,
not with ease,
but with vision:

Comfort ye.

For the crooked shall be made straight.
The exile shall come home.
Not because the world relents—
but because God does.

Because the Eternal has entered time.
And in that mystery,
we find our place again.

THE OTHER ORDER
After Chapter 3 – "The Paradox of the Beatitudes"

> *"Blessed are the poor in spirit, for theirs is the kingdom of heaven. Blessed are those who mourn, for they will be comforted.* — *Matthew 5:3–4 (NRSVA)*

He lifted his eyes—
not to the sky,
But to us.

To the weary and weatherworn,
to those the world passes by,
to those whose hands bear calluses
but not crowns,
whose hearts ache with the cost of kindness.

And he said:
Blessed.

Not because we were strong,
or certain,
or safe—
but because we were seen.

Blessed is humankind,
not in spite of our sorrow,
but through it.

Blessed are the poor,
whose hunger teaches them to pray.
Blessed are the mourners,
whose grief breaks open the heart of God.

Blessed are the meek,
who carry the earth quietly
as if it were sacred.

This is the scandal:
To be blessed may look like being forgotten.
To be chosen may feel like being cast out.

But the world that mocks humanity
is already passing.
And the order that exalts humanity
is already rising.

We live in two orders:
one that crowns the powerful,
and one that lifts the lowly.
One that rewards the winners,
and one that remembers the wounded.
One that fears the truth,
and one that is truth.

Woe to those
who cannot imagine joy beyond laughter,
or hunger beyond food.
Woe to those
whose fullness leaves no room for mercy.

For there is a poverty
that opens the door to another kingdom—
and a wealth
that seals it shut.

He looked into our eyes—
not through us,
but into us—
and said:

Humankind is not forgotten.
We are embraced in a realm
we cannot yet see.

Rejoice.
Not in spite of the world,
but because a greater order has arisen.

Because we were always known.

THE TWO SERVANTS
After Chapter 4 — "The Two Servants of Jahweh"

> *"I call you by your name, I surname you, though you do*
> *not know me. I am the Lord, and there is no other."*
> *— Isaiah 45:4–5 (NRSVA)*

We heard a voice—
not thundering from a throne,
but rising from the rubble,
quiet as breath
through broken cities.

Not the voice of kings,
though it named them.
Not the voice of priests,
though it judged the altars.
Not the voice of victors,
but of a servant
hidden among the wounded.

Come forward, it said.
Bring your proofs,
your metal gods and market plans,
your forged thrones and painted dreams.
Let them speak.
Let them tell us
What truth survives the shaking?

But there was only silence,
draped in the wreckage
of our certainty.

Then we saw one rise—
not humble, not holy,
but chosen still—
a ruler who did not know
the name he served.
His hands shattered chains
he could not see.
And through him,
freedom opened a path.

But, this is not redemption.
And he is not the one we follow.

There is another.
Whom we must not miss.
He bore no sword,
only silence.
No empire,
only mercy.

He did not come to conquer,
but to be wounded.
To carry our grief
without defense.

He was the servant
whose strength was sorrow,
whose power was endurance.
The One who bore
what others broke.

There are always two:
one who builds with the sword,
and one who becomes
the cornerstone.

And the question is not
which will triumph—
for both are held
in a story greater than their will.

The question is:
To whom do we listen?

Where do we turn
when history stammers
and every idol is silent?

Not to the voice of dominance,
but to the one
whose blood speaks
when the world goes quiet.

The servant will rise.
Not Cyrus—
but the one he never knew.

And history,
in all its trembling,
will bow
to the one
who bore it.

YOU ARE IN THE ETERNAL NOW
After Chapter 5 – "Meditation: The Mystery of Time"

> *"He has made everything suitable for its time; moreover he has put a sense of eternity into their minds…"*— *Ecclesiastes 3:11 (NRSVA)*

There comes an insight, a moment
when time no longer transports us—
it scatters us. Time stops in hesitation.
The hours course like water,
the days and nights wear thin.
We chase what was,
reach toward what may come,
and lose the ground beneath our feet.

We ask:
Where is the present,
if the past is gone
and the future not yet?

We speak the word *now*—
but by the time it leaves our lips,
it already belongs to memory.

Do not despair.
This is not failure.
Time dissolves into a whisper.
A voice we once heard.
This is the mystery.

We are not trapped
in the river's sorrowful stream.
We are pierced by eternity.

Not the ticking of clocks,
but the stillness between them—
that is where we are met.
That is where God speaks.

The eternal now is not illusion.
It is the point where time is touched
by something deeper still.

And so,
when we feel hurried or hollowed,
when we are driven toward a future
we do not yet know,
let us stop.

Let this moment be enough.
Let it open like a flower in our hands.
Let it remind us that
what matters most
is already here.

We are not passing away.
We are being met—
by the Presence who holds all time
and yet
is never bound by it.

We are in the eternal now.

WE ARE KNOWN

After Chapter 6 – "The Escape from God"

> *"O Lord, you have searched me and known me. You know when I sit down and when I rise up; you discern my thoughts from far away." — Psalm 139:1–2 (NRSVA)*

We hesitate to be known and seen—
even when there is an ache within—
when our prayers feel too loud,
our thoughts too exposed,
our hearts too restless to bear their own witness.

We long to disappear—
into the quiet hum of doing,
or the deeper hush of not caring.

We flee into our labor,
into our distractions,
into the noise that drowns the ache.

But even there—
even in forgetting—
we are known.

We build gods in our own image:
harmless, distant, well-behaved.
But not the real God.

Not the One whose gaze
undoes pretense
and calls the soul by name.

We descend into despair
or ascend into performance,
trying to outpace
what waits for us in the stillness.

But we are known.
Even our hiding
is held in the hand
of the One we hide from.

We rage, we retreat,
we resist the witness of grace.
But grace does not flinch.
It stays.
It sees.
It loves.
Not the mask.
Not the story.
But the self
we dare not name.

And when we can bear it no longer—
when we come again to the silence,
the wilderness within—
we may hear a voice not accusing,
but calling.

Search me.
Try me.
See what is hidden,
and lead me toward the light
I once feared
would undo me.
For the light does not destroy.
It reveals.
It restores.

We are known.
And still—
we are loved.

WE ARE CALLED TO THE DEPTH
After Chapter 7 – "The Depth of Existence" Part I

> *"Deep calls to deep at the thunder of your cataracts; all your waves and your billows have gone over me."* — *Psalm 42:7 (NRSVA)*

There are moments
when the surface beneath us
is no longer firm—
can no longer hold—
when even joy feels thin,
when we must dive deeper
and what we called truth
begins to tremble under our feet.

A stirring
of the Spirit begins,
not loud but low,
not above,
but within—
calling us deeper.

Deeper than opinion,
deeper than fear,
deeper than the polished phrases
we use to hide our ache.

We cannot answer with borrowed words.
Not this time, nor across time.

We must descend—
into the cavern of our being,
to the indwelling spaces,
where the questions echo still,
unanswered
and unafraid.

This is not escape.
This is invitation.

Do not fear the descent.
It is not complexity that awaits,
but clarity—
stripped bare of deception
where illusion dissolves.

We will weep there,
perhaps without knowing why.
We will see
that suffering carves space
for truth to enter.

And truth, when it comes,
will not flatter.
It will not spare us.
But it will hold us.

For the soul's descent
is not a fall—
but a return.

We are not being punished.
We are being uncovered.

And if we remain long enough,
if we do not flee back to surface certainties,
we may hear another voice—
quiet with joy,
rooted in mercy,
speaking from the still place
where God dwells.

The world is deep.
And we are not meant
to stand in the shallow tide.
We were made for what endures.

There is pain in this breaking open—
but there is something deeper still.
Not comfort without cost,
but joy that has passed through fire.

This is not the end.
This is the threshold.
We are called to the depth.

And in the depth,
God is already there,
waiting.

YOU ARE HELD IN JOY
After Chapter 7 – "The Depth of Existence" Part II

> *These things God has revealed to us through the Spirit; for the Spirit searches everything, even the depths of God. — 1 Corinthians 2:10 (NRSVA)*

There are seasons
when sorrow sits beside us—
not loudly,
but with the weight of an old friend.
When silence fills the room
and joy seems a word
from another language.

We wonder
if it ever belonged to us,
or if we dreamed it long ago
when the world felt lighter.

We are not wrong to grieve.
The world is broken.
Our hearts crack in places
that cannot be patched
with platitudes.

But wait.

Do not rise too quickly
from the ache.
Do not mistake silence
for absence.

There is something here—
deeper than sorrow,
older than fear,
more patient than despair.

This is not the joy of distraction
or denial.
This is joy born in shadow,
joy that does not blink
in the face of loss.

Joy that says:
Even here—
especially here—
you are not alone.

Joy that has tasted ash
and still sings.

Joy that remembers every tear
and is not undone by them.

It does not erase pain.
It walks beside it.

We are held in this joy—
not the fleeting kind,
but the kind that endures
because it has endured.

It is written into the deep.
It is the last word
beneath the silence.

And when we rise again,
when our feet find the path
through the forest of sorrow,
we will know:

We were never abandoned.
We are held in joy.

YOU ARE DUST, AND YET
After Chapter 8 – "On the Transitoriness of Life"

"So teach us to number our days, that we may gain a wise heart." — Psalm 90:12 (NRSVA)

We are dust—
and yet we remember eternity.

Something in us reaches
beyond the veil of days,
toward a measure not our own—
a rhythm untouched by decay,
a home we cannot name
but never forget.

We feel it
when the wind turns cold,
when the leaves fall
and are not gathered again.
We know it
when joy fades too quickly,
when even long years
end in a whisper.

From dust we came,
to dust we return—
this we do not deny.
But still,
our hearts resist the grave.

Why do we mourn what is natural?
Why does something eternal
cry out from within
when a child dies
or wisdom fades into silence?

We are not only dust.
We are longing,
we are memory,
we are the ache
that time cannot contain.

And in our rebellion
against the silence of the tomb,
we pray—
not only with our lips,
but with our weariness:

Teach us to number our days,
that we may gain
a heart of wisdom.

We do not ask for a longer life—
but a truer one.

A life that sings
even in sorrow.
A life that matters
even in dying.

We hope for mercy.
We plead for joy
where affliction has been.
We dream of a day
when our labor will not
be washed away
by the tide.

And still—
we dare to say:
Relent, O Eternal.
Let not wrath
be the final word.
Let glory touch the dust again.

We are dust.
But we are also
the cry that rises from dust
toward the heart of God.

And in that cry—
not denial,
not despair—
but the trembling cry
of longing remembered,
wisdom begins.

There is a place
where sorrow bends
toward something more.
Where mercy becomes
what judgment never could be.
Where every sigh is heard.
And God becomes
our dwelling place—
again.

THE EARTH STILL SPEAKS
After Chapter 9 – The Salvation of Nature

> *The heavens are telling the glory of God,*
> *and the firmament proclaims his handiwork.*
> *² Day to day pours forth speech,*
> *and night to night declares knowledge.*
> *— Psalm 19:1-2 (NRSVA)*

The earth is not silent.
Not yet.

Though our machines outshout the trees,
and our cities forget the song of rivers,
still the earth speaks.

It speaks in silence,
in shadow,
in the hush between lightning and leaf.

It speaks through the ache of the branch,
the stretch of root,
the prayer of stone.

Day unto day pours out speech—
not in syllables,
but in light.
Night unto night reveals knowledge
in stars that do not perform,
and wind that sings only for those who still listen.

Do we hear it?
The hymn hidden in the lilies,
the groan in the belly of the lion,
the longing in the hush before snow.

Creation waits—
not passively,
but with laboring hope.
She remembers the garden.
And so do we.

We, too, groan—
not as masters,
but as creatures.
Not as spectators,
but as kin.

For we are not saved apart from the world,
but with it.

Not as disembodied spirits
drifting in some sterile heaven,
but as dust transfigured,
flesh glorified,
matter made mercy.

This is why the river flows
from the throne of God and the Lamb.
This is why the tree bears fruit
in every season.
Because even time
will be healed.

And the leaves?
The leaves are for the healing of the nations.
For those who forgot to listen.
For those who still might remember.

So return.
Not as owner,
but as child.
Take off your shoes.
Kneel in the grove.
Let the soil speak.

Watch the fox walk without sound.
Watch the heron stand without fear.
Let your soul be restored
by the God who walked in the garden,
and never truly left.

Perhaps then,
we will remember
how to walk with Him again.

YOU ARE UNDONE AND MADE WHOLE
After Chapter 10 – "The Experience of the Holy" Part I

> *"Woe is me! I am lost… Then a seraph touched my mouth*
> *with a coal… and I heard the Lord say, 'Whom shall I send?'*
> *I said, 'Here am I; send me!'"* — Isaiah 6:5–8 (NRSVA)

There are moments
when we are no longer safe—
when silence enters the sanctuary
and something vast and veiled
draws near.

We do not see the face of God.
Only a shadow,
a trembling threshold,
a voice like fire in our bones.

And still,
we know.
We have entered the holy.

We are not proud in that place.
We do not speak in clever tones.
We say,
"Woe is me. I am undone."

And yet—
it is there
we are made whole.

It wasn't our cleanliness—
it was mercy
that made the coal burn holy.
From an altar not made by hands,
it seared a clean heart into us—
and left us forgiven.

Do not seek certainty.
Seek the shaking.
Do not ask to be worthy.
You will not be.

But you will be chosen.

You will hear the question
no one else hears—
"Whom shall I send?"
And somehow—
with trembling voice,
with a heart undone—
you will say,
"Here am I. Send me."

And that yes
will be the beginning
of a long undoing.
For what is holy does not flatter.
And what is true
does not come wrapped in welcome.

We will speak,
and they may not listen.
We will love,
and still be rejected.

This is the cost
of the prophet's call.
This is the fire
that purifies.

Yet still—
the vision remains:

Glory—not in isolation,
but wed to justice.
Not majesty alone,
but majesty with mercy.

No idol made in our image,
but the God of Hosts—
who breaks us open,
and in mercy,
unmakes and remakes us
whole again.

So when we are undone,
let us not flee.

For only what is undone
can be truly made whole.

THE HOLY SHALL NOT BE TAMED
After Chapter 10 – "The Experience of the Holy" Part II

> *In the year that King Uzziah died, I saw the Lord sitting on a throne, high and lofty; and the hem of his robe filled the temple. ² Seraphs were in attendance above him; each had six wings: with two they covered their faces, and with two they covered their feet, and with two they flew. — Isaiah 6:1-2 (NRSVA)*

In the year everything fell apart,
we saw—
or rather, we did not see—
but trembled before a presence
we could not comprehend.

A veil of smoke filled the air.
The ground beneath us groaned
as though the foundations of the world
had remembered how to cry out.

Even now,
some part of us still quivers
with what cannot be named.

Holy. Holy. Holy—
we heard it,
each time breaking something in us
we did not know was there.

It was not comfort.
It was not ceremony.
It was not "religion."

It was fire.

The kind that sings in cedar
and scorches the tongue.
The kind that does not explain itself.
The kind that breaks us
so it can send us.

We tried to speak,
but there was only ash.
We said: Unclean.
Unready.
Undone.

Not only for our sins,
but for our shallow vision—
the way we mistook God's silence
for absence,
or worse, approval.

Then a coal was taken from the altar.
A flame pressed to our lips
and did not consume—
only what had to go.

Then came the Voice—
not thunder,
but breaking:

Whom shall I send?

And we—
not knowing where,
not knowing how—
answered with our lives:

Here we are. Send us.

And God did.

Not with words that would console,
but with a Word
too holy for compromise,
too sharp for easy comfort,
too wild to be held in safe hands.

This Word exposes idols
by naming them.
It turns friends into questioners,
and power into dust.

It is not a plan.
It is a wound—
through which God enters history.

How long, O Lord?

Until the cities fall silent.
Until the last illusion has crumbled.
Until only the stump remains.
Until the remnant
learns to listen.
Until the seed
beneath the soil
trembles again with hope.

THE YOKE THAT FREES
After Chapter 11 – "The Yoke of Religion"

> *"Come to me, all you that are weary and are carrying heavy burdens, and I will give you rest. ²⁹ Take my yoke upon you, and learn from me; for I am gentle and humble in heart, and you will find rest for your souls. ³⁰ For my yoke is easy, and my burden is light." — Matthew 11:28, 30 (NRSVA)*

There is a weight
we were never meant to carry.
It comes as a whisper:
Be perfect. Be pure. Be sure.

And so we try—
with creeds memorized,
with prayers recited until they crack,
with doctrines defended
like shields against doubt.

We strive.
We serve.
We strain to be enough.

We build our sanctuaries
on should and must,
we labor beneath the names of God
but forget how to rest in them.

Even our goodness grows tired.

And then—
a voice.

No decree, no command—
nor rules carved on stone tablets,
simply a quiet invitation to:
Come as you are.

Not come and believe.
Not come and obey.
Just—Come.

The burden is not our sin.
It is the scaffolding of striving.
It is the voice that tells us
grace must be earned
and love must be proven.

But here is the Christ
who says:
My yoke is easy.
My burden is light.

And when we brace for a ledger,
He gives us bread.
When we expect condemnation,
He sits beside us in silence.

Not religion remade,
but religion released—
unlearned in mercy,
undone by grace.

Not a holier climb, rather faith
transformed by the arms of One
who descended every rung
to meet us where we already are.

We are not yoked
to duty,
but to delight.
Not to shame,
but to love.

And when we say yes,
even faintly—
when we lay down
the burden of proving—
our striving stills.

Not because we finally let go,
or found the perfect
rhythm to be still,
but because rest
found its way to us
in the quiet between breaths—
and stayed,
even when we didn't know
how to welcome it.

THE THREAD THAT HOLDS
After Chapter 12 – "The Meaning of Providence"

> *For I am convinced that neither death, nor life, nor angels, nor rulers, nor things present, nor things to come, nor powers,* [39] *nor height, nor depth, nor anything else in all creation, will be able to separate us from the love of God in Christ Jesus our Lord. — Romans 8:38–39 (NRSVA)*

There are days
when the sky breaks open
with grief,
and no comfort is given.
When hunger marches in rags,
and cruelty wears a crown,
and prayer feels like
breathing underwater.

On those days,
when Providence is most silent,
we remember:

It was never the promise
of happy endings
that made this holy—
but the fierce thread of love
that holds
when all else unravels.

What holds us isn't a plan—
it's the Presence that abides.

It is a vow
of certainty.

That even now—
with death falling from the heavens,
with refugees wandering roads of ash,
with children born into sorrow—
even now
we are not abandoned.

Providence is not the hand
that prevents the blow,
but the hand
that holds us afterward
and will not let go.

It is the Christ
who descends
into the horror
and still says:
Nothing can separate you.

Not angels.
Not powers.
Not height.
Not depth.
Not even despair
dressed in reason.

In the pit
where meaning dies,
Love remains.
Love remakes.
Love raises.

And so we live,
not by sight—
but by the audacity
to trust
what cannot be undone:

That in Christ
we are held
by a grace
stronger than ruin,
and more final
than death.

THROUGH THE GLASS
After Chapter 13 – "Knowledge Through Love" Part I

> *If I speak in the tongues of mortals and of angels, but do not have love, I am a noisy gong or a clanging cymbal.* [2] *And if I have prophetic powers, and understand all mysteries and all knowledge, and if I have all faith, so as to remove mountains, but do not have love, I am nothing.* [3] *If I give away all my possessions, and if I hand over my body so that I may boast,*[a] *but do not have love, I gain nothing.* — 1 Corinthians 13:1-3 (NRSVA)

We live among fragments—
not ruins of what was,
but glimpses of what will be.

Each thought a splinter,
each truth a shard,
light caught on the edges
of something we can't yet hold.

We do not know—
not fully.
Not yet.

Even our finest words,
our richest prophecies,
our most radiant ideas,
fade like mist
before the mountain of love.

For love is not sentiment.
It is not escape.
It is the clarity
that comes when one soul
dares to know another
without demand,
without disguise.

We do not see by reason alone.
We are not made whole by certainty.
It is love that sees
into the wound
and stays.

Love listens
long enough to hear
what the silence hides.

We know in part.
We live in part.
We are broken in part.

And still—
within the riddle,
the answer lives.

There is a knowing
that does not conquer,
but communes.
It moves not from proof to proof,
but from heart to heart.

The child in us
still presses against the glass,
still reaches for the shape
beyond the veil.

But one day,
the mirror will turn.
And we will see—
not as idea,
not as image,
but face to face.

The fragments
will not vanish.
They will sing.

And we will know—
because we are known.
And we will love—
because we are love.

YOU ARE FULLY KNOWN
After Chapter 13 – "Knowledge Through Love" Part II

> *For now we see in a mirror, dimly,*[a] *but then we will see face to face. Now I know only in part; then I will know fully, even as I have been fully known.* [13] *And now faith, hope, and love abide, these three; and the greatest of these is love.* — *1 Corinthians 13:12-13 (NRSVA)*

There is an agony in time
when all we know will feel like
broken shards—
pieces of a truth
we no longer see
a truth too deep to reconcile.

We speak in partial sentences.
We live in partial light.
We walk through mirrors
that show only what's missing.

We wonder
if we were ever whole.
If knowing was ever possible.
If love is just a word
we are learning too late.

But even now—
in the scattered shards,
in the silence—
we are fully known.

Known not by measure,
not by achievement,
not by what we understand,
but by love.

Love that sees the shattered mirror
and does not turn away.
Love that waits in the riddle.
Love that holds us
when we cannot hold ourselves.

We are not problems to solve.
We are not equations to prove.
We are not failures
because we are unfinished.

We are known.

And we are not alone in this.
Every soul we meet
is its own mystery.
Every face we love
holds a question
we do not need to answer
to remain.

All our certainties will vanish.
All our languages will fall silent.
All our wisdom
will return to dust.

But love—
love will remain.

Love is the only knowledge
that does not disappear.

So let the fragments be.
Let them fall
like petals or prayers.

What remains
is not only what was whole,
but what has been made holy
through breaking.

We are the ones
who walk among the shards,
who gather the scattered light,
who carry the ache of the vessels
and the hope of their repair.

To be known is not to be solved—
it is to be seen
in our unfinished beauty,
to be held
by the One
who shines through every fracture.

And in that light,
we are called by name.
And in that calling,
we begin to become whole.

DOING THE TRUTH
After Chapter 14 – Paul Tillich's "Doing the Truth"

> *But those who do what is true come to the light, so that it may be clearly seen that their deeds have been done in God.* — John 3:21 (NRSVA)

We do not live truth
with words alone—
nor with creeds we recite
in borrowed voices.

Truth is not stored
in scroll or system.
It is not framed
in certainty.

It walks.
It weeps.
It kneels beside the wounded.
It enters the room
where justice has been delayed
and does not leave.

We do the truth
not to defend an argument,
not to win a debate,
but because a flame
has risen in our chest,

as *Resurrection*—
and we cannot look away
from what has been revealed.

Truth is not proven.
It is practiced.
Not imposed,
but embodied.

To do the truth
is to become transparent
to the Light that seeks
every hidden place—
not to shame,
but to heal.

It is to let our lives
become windows,
not mirrors—
so that what shines through
is not our certainty,
but our surrender.

We do not carry truth
as possession.
We let it carry us.

And when we stumble,
when we fail,
when we fall short—
we rise again,
because the truth we do
is not ours to own,
but ours to trust.

So let us walk
as those who have seen the fire
and not turned away.

Let us walk
as those who know
truth is never abstract
when love takes it seriously.

Let us walk
as those whose lives
are becoming an answer
the world cannot dismiss.

THEOLOGIAN
After Chapter 15 – "Theologian" Part I

For we are the aroma of Christ to God among those who are being saved and among those who are perishing; [16] *to the one a fragrance from death to death, to the other a fragrance from life to life. Who is sufficient for these things? — 2 Corinthians 2:15-16 (NRSVA)*

Not by mastery,
nor by the ease of speech,
nor by a tongue
that names the Spirit
as if it were its own—

but by the ache of unknowing,
by the tremble that follows
one honest question:
Who are You, O God,
and who are we
that You are mindful of us?

To speak of You
is not to explain—
but to burn.
We did not choose this path.
It found us—
in the place where answers die
and silence becomes a sanctuary.

Even there—
especially there—
a whisper rose:

Not cursed is He,
but Christ.
Not foolishness,
but foundation.

We do not always believe.
But we cannot leave the question.
It follows us
into every word,
every breath,
every act of naming.

We do not know if we are wise.
But we know this longing.
And in that longing,
we are not alone.

If the word of wisdom is given,
it is not ours—
but gift.
If truth appears,
it arrives through tears.

We believe, Lord.
Help our unbelief.

So call us theologians,
not for what we claim,
but for what we
cannot forsake—
the trembling,
the witness.
The sacred hunger
to speak where the
Incarnate Word,
the *Logos*—
has spoken our name first.

AS THOUGH WEAK
After Chapter 15 – "Theologian" Part II

> *"To those outside the law I became as one outside the law (though I am not free from God's law but am under Christ's law) so that I might win those outside the law. ²² To the weak I became weak, so that I might win the weak. I have become all things to all people, so that I might by any means save some."* — *1 Corinthians 9:21-22 (NRSVA)*

Not to stand above,
but beside.
Not to proclaim from strength,
but to listen through the ache.

To the idealist, we bore the shape of dreams,
though we knew their breaking.
To the realist, we wore the dust of earth,
while we carried the Pentecostal flame.

We became what they were —
not to flatter,
not to persuade by pretense,
but to stand where they stood,
so we could speak from within
what truth had already begun.

We did not possess it.
The truth possessed us.
And even then,
we trembled.

The theologian is not the one who is right —
but the one
who, being wrong a thousand times,
still cannot stop asking.

To the weak, we became weak.
Not to rescue,
but to know.
Not to instruct,
but to suffer-with.

Strength?
It is not mine.
Only the courage to name
our unknowing.

Only the grace
to sit in silence
until the Word
speaks again.

We do not build arguments.
We build bridges
with trembling hands,
so love may cross
from one heart to another
unannounced.

And when we speak,
before we speak,
may we pause in peace
to remember.

To be as those
who came before us,
who listened first
to the weeping of the world
and the whisper of the Spirit.

TO THE UNKNOWN GOD
After Chapter 15 – "Theologian" Part III

> *"What therefore you worship as unknown, this I proclaim to you."* — *Acts 17:23 (NRSV)*

We stood where the questions gather—
on the hill where reason burns like incense,
where altars rise to every answer
but the one that stays unnamed.

We did not come to conquer doubt
or bind the mind with certainties.
We came to name
what already burns
beneath the asking.

For those—who wonder.
For those—who run.
For those—who rage.

He is not far
from any one of us.
Even in exile,
even in disguise,
even when we kneel at the wrong altar—
still, the breath within our breath
comes from the One
we do not yet name.

The idols glitter—
but they cannot speak.
They cannot bleed.
They cannot rise.

And yet One has come—
not to shame our seeking,
but to answer it.
Not with a sword,
but a wound.
Not with triumph,
but with truth.

He is not a theory.
He is a man.
Not above suffering,
but risen through it.

He is the face behind the veil,
the voice within our silence,
the judge who bears our judgment.

The world may mock resurrection.
Some still do.
But others—
others hear, and stay.

And so we stand,
as all true theologians must—
not above,
but within,
naming the grace
that was there
before the question.

And we say:
The God you seek,
the God you fear,
the God you dare not name—
has already found you.
And He is love.

WE BEAR WITNESS
After Chapter 15 – "The Theologian" Part IV

> *"In him we live and move and have our being"; as even some*
> *of your own poets have said, 'For we too are his offspring.'"*
> — *Acts 17:28 (NRSVA)*

We walked the hill with Paul,
beneath the carved gods of reason and stone,
where truth lay veiled beneath our clever altars—
"To the Unknown"—we had named Him so.

We thought we searched alone,
but now we see:
He was never far.
We lived in Him, moved in Him,
had our being—
even in our blindness.

We have worshiped shadows,
imagined gods in our own image,
offered incense to our fears,
and lit fires to light our own escape
from the silence that was never silence at all.

But grace speaks through the Logos still:
not to condemn,
but to awaken.
To turn us from our lesser gods
and bring us near to the One
in whom all names dissolve into love.

We have felt
the quivering moment—
the quickening of flesh,
when the Holy Spirit descends.
When the truth becomes flesh again,
when the Risen One walks among our questions,
and we are not mocked,
but met.

So let us answer, not with certainty,
but with witness.
Let us name the paradox,
not to wound with mystery,
but to reveal the wound that heals:
Christ among us.

We are not far
from the One we cannot name.
We are His offspring still.
And we bear witness,
in fragments of faith,
to the God who speaks
even from unknown altars
across many traditions.

WE WHO GROAN IN THE SPIRIT

After Chapter 16 – "The Witness of the Spirit to the Spirit"

> *"Likewise the Spirit helps us in our weakness; for we do not know how to pray as we ought, but that very Spirit intercedes with sighs too deep for words."* — Romans 8:26 (NRSVA)

We walk this world as those who wait—
for what, we do not always know.
Our breath is prayer without words,
our longing deeper than thought.
The sky itself groans with us,
as if all creation were exhaling
the ache of becoming.

We do not stand alone in this.
We are not left to our own silence.
There is One who sighs within our sighs,
who kneels within our weakness,
who prays through our unspoken cries—
the Spirit, searching hearts
more tenderly than we ever could.

We say, "Abba," and tremble,
not because we are sure,
but because something in us
remembers being held.
Not by the law that condemned,
but by the love that descended—
into flesh like ours, into death like ours—
to make us children again.

We have lived under the weight of the law,
its mirror showing us all we are not.
We have resented it,
even as we bowed to its truth.
We have tried to flee,
only to find ourselves still captive
to desire unbound, to power unending.

Yet even here,
the Spirit does not depart.
It enters the fractures.
It moves in the places we cannot move.
And when we fall silent,
when we can no longer name hope,
it sings for us—
with groanings too deep for speech.

We are not what we shall be.
We have not yet arrived.
But we are not what we were.
For something eternal breathes in us now—
a life not our own,
a peace not of this world,
a love that says:

"You are mine.
You always were.
You always will be."

So we listen.
And in the stillness,
we remember:
We are the children of God.

WE SAY: THOU ART THE CHRIST
After Chapter 17 – "He Who is the Christ"

> *He asked them, "But who do you say that I am?" Peter answered him, "You are the Messiah."*—Mark 8:29 (NRSVA)

We walked with Him once,
not on the road to Caesarea Philippi,
but along other roads—
through grief, through questions,
through the strange silence
between hope and heartbreak.

He turned to us and asked,
as He once asked the Twelve,
"Who do you say that I am?"
And we wanted to answer
with what we had been taught—
a prophet, a teacher,
a light among many lights.

But something in His gaze
searched deeper than memory.
It looked past the borrowed names,
the old longings for glory,
for a king who might rescue us
by might or by miracle.

And so, trembling, we said it—
not because we fully understood,
but because His presence
made the words truer than our doubt:
Thou art the Christ.

Not the Christ we imagined—
robed in triumph,
ushering in peace with a sword.
No, not that one.
But the One who bears
rejection without retaliation,
whose power is revealed
in suffering freely chosen,
in wounds that refuse to hate.

He silenced our attempts to define Him.
Our confusion would not enthrone him.
Instead, He showed us
the way the Divine must walk:
through the jeering of councils,
through the silence of death,
through the stone rolled away
not in thunder, but in grace.

We have tried to follow since.
We have preached and sung His name.
But too often we name Him
without awe, without trembling—
forgetting what it means
to call Jesus the Christ.

We forget what it means
to call Jesus the Christ—
that to say it
is to follow where we fear to go,
to love past every wound,
to lose and still belong.

So now, again, we fall silent—
not out of fear,
but out of reverence.
For this is no ordinary claim.
This is a cry of the heart
before the mystery of God made flesh.

We say:
You are the Christ.
Not because we understand You,
but because You have known us—
in our betrayal, our longing,
our resistance, our hope.

And still You walk beside us.
Still You carry the Cross.
Still You rise.

We say:
Thou art the Christ.

WE WHO WAIT
After Chapter 18 – "Waiting"

> *"I wait for the Lord, my soul waits, and in His word I hope."*
> *— Psalm 130:5 (NRSV)*

We wait for the Lord—
not in stillness without ache,
but with souls stretched thin
like watchers before the dawn,
aching for a light
we have not yet seen
but know must come.

We wait not because we are idle,
but because we have been seized
by something beyond our naming,
a whisper of the eternal
woven into time.
We do not possess God—
how could we?
Not in creed, not in church,
not in scripture well-worn
nor in the sanctified silence of prayer.
We cannot carry Him in doctrine,
nor keep Him in the lines of a sermon.
He breaks our containers,
escapes our conclusions,
transcends our best intentions.

And so—we wait.

We wait
as those who have glimpsed
what we cannot grasp,
as those who have been wounded
by hope,
and yet
do not turn away.

We wait
in tension and trust,
in the humility of knowing
that our not-knowing
may be the truest form of faith.

We wait, not with despair,
but with longing—
for the God who will not be possessed,
but who comes,
even now,
in the spaces between breath and belief.

We wait,
and in our waiting,
we are changed.

We are not empty—
but held,
by the very One
for whom we wait.

YOU ARE ACCEPTED
After Chapter 19 – "You Are Accepted"

Sometimes at that moment a wave of light breaks into our darkness, and it is as though a voice were saying: "You are accepted." —Paul Tillich

There will come a time in your life
when what may be is a path you
must decide upon—purposely or intuitively—
influenced by both your conscious
and unconscious mind.

One side will come from
what you already know
about yourself, how something
makes you smile in a world
that always makes sense.

The other side will come from
what is sad and broken and
askew within the world—chaos,
unaware of the self's unlimited
potential, and how your thoughts shape
everything.

The world you live in
is coming from you.
What I can tell you from
my own experience is:

do not fret or feel threatened.
Simply be.

Being itself
is the reason you are here.
It is the reason for living.

Your life is a gift, and your
only obligation within it
is to live that life fully,
and let everything else unfold
graciously before your eyes.

You do
not have to question why.
You do not need to fear.

You only need to accept
that you are accepted—
in all that you are and will
be—by something greater
than yourself.

Even if—
especially if—
it is something
you cannot name now.

Do not even try.
For grace may strike when
your need is greatest.
You will name it later.

And do not
expect that you will be
better than before, or
believe more than before.

It can happen this way.

You can love your life,
and be transformed
by the Ground of Being—
God—the groundlessness and
openness of all creation arising,
being itself—this mystery.

BORN IN A GRAVE
After Chapter 20 – "Born in a Grave"

"You have put me in the depths of the Pit, in the regions dark and deep." — *Psalm 88:6 (NRSVA)*

There are places
where even breath must hide—
where earth closes in like a second skin,
and the living learn to wait
among the dead.

In Wilna, Poland, in the shadow
of the holocaust a child was born
in a grave—
not metaphor, not symbol,
but stone and linen,
a mother's trembling womb
wrapped in silence and frost.

The gravedigger,
eighty years old and aching,
held the child in the folds
of a burial shroud,
and whispered,
O God—
is this the Messiah?
Who else, but the Messiah,
can be born in a grave?

But there was no milk.
Only tears,
and three days later,
only silence.
No halo.
No star.
Just a child
fading into the dark
with the others.

This too,
is gospel.

Before the rising,
there is the sealed stone.
Before the angel speaks,
there are the guards
and the grave,
and a world so wounded
it cannot bear
even the scent of hope
without flinching.

Let us not rush
past the buried.
Let us not speak
of resurrection
as if it were a given.

He was buried.
He—
not a part of Him,
not just His body,
but the whole
of who He was.

Buried,
and the stone rolled shut.

Only this makes
the rising
matter.

Only this allows us
to believe
that the grave
is not the end.

Not every story is born
in a manger.
Some begin in tombs.
And if the Christ
is to rise at all,
then He must first
be sealed away—
with us,
for us—
in the dark.

And if there is a voice
still daring to hope,
may it rise
like that old man's prayer:

O God,
hast Thou finally sent
the Messiah?
For who else
can be born
in a grave?

THE DESTRUCTION OF DEATH

After Chapter 21 – "The Destruction of Death"

"...that through death he might destroy the one who has the power of death, that is, the devil, [15] and free those who all their lives were held in slavery by the fear of death." — Hebrews 2:14–15 (NRSVA)

We are born knowing
what we cannot name—
the thread of death
already woven
into the loom of breath.

It moves through the marrow,
familiar as pulse,
a shadow cast
before any sun
has risen.

And yet—
something in us resists.
We bury the thought
beneath busy days
and hymns that end in major chords.

Still, it waits—
not at the end,
but within the middle,
between the words we say
and the fears we dare not speak.

For it is not death alone
that binds us,
but the fear of it.
Not the loss of breath,
but the ache
that we might deserve
to be forgotten.

So we run—
not from dust,
but from guilt,
from the knowledge
that our separation
is chosen,
and yet not chosen.

The bondage is this:
that we are both
mortal and eternal,

finite and infinite,
and we have forgotten
how to hold both truths
without despair.

But He came,
not as a ghost
or angelic fire,
but clothed in blood and crying,
to destroy the thing
that destroys us—
not death,
but the power of it.

He came to take on
what we fear most,
to meet us in the Gethsemane
of our own trembling,
to be afraid with us
and still
go on.

This is how Eternity came:
not to explain away the grave,
but to enter it—
and rise.

Not to take death
from the world,
but to draw the sting
from the wound
and name the wound
holy.

This is Christmas:
not sentiment,
but salvation;
not decoration,
but deliverance
from fear.

*Why? Because
we fail to see
what Christ imagines.*

YOU ARE BEING MADE NEW
After Chapter 22 – "Behold, I Am Doing a New Thing"

> *"I am doing a new thing; now it springs forth, do you not perceive it?"* — Isaiah 43:19 (NRSVA)

A time comes when
The old will no longer hold you—
Not because it is gone,
But because it is breaking.

You may not know what is crumbling.
Only that what once steadied you
Now seems hollow.
You may try to restore it—
Patch the garment, preserve the form—
But it will not hold.

You will stand in the ruins
Of things once beautiful,
Once vital.
And you will weep.
You may try to remember
What it felt like to believe
That the old was enough.

But hear this:
The weeping is holy.
The breaking is blessed.

Do not fear the wilderness
That rises around you.
Do not fear the desert
That opens beneath your feet.

For even here,
Especially here—
A river begins to flow.

You are being made new.

Not by willpower.
Not by your plans.
Not even by your hope.

The new does not come by force—
It arrives in surrender.
It appears in forgotten corners,
In neglected soil,
In the soul you thought
Had dried beyond recovery.

You are being made new
When the burden of the past
No longer has the final word.

When forgiveness finds its way
Through the cracked places
And softens the stone
Into flesh.

You are being made new
Because Love is always new.
And Love is always now.

Do you not perceive it?

Even now—
In the silence between endings,
In the shadows of forgetting,
In the ache that will not name itself—
It is springing to light.

Be still.
Be ready.
You are not alone.
You are not abandoned.

You are being made new.

ACKNOWLEDGMENTS & THANKS

I want to thank the friends, poets, priests, pastors, teachers, and contemplatives who offered encouragement and insight throughout the writing of this book. Your listening hearts and thoughtful questions reminded me again and again that theology is never merely an idea—it is a lived conversation. Your presence helped me welcome the silences between the words, and your companionship made this journey less solitary and more sacred.

These poems are not theological commentary. They are not paraphrases or poetic restatements of Paul Tillich's sermons. They are responses—written in the margins of his wisdom, in the echo of his voice. They are what happens when one listens deeply to a soul who dared to speak of grace without condition, of courage in the face of despair, and of God as the ground of being—the hidden foundation holding all things in creation together.

This book enters into dialogue with Tillich's *The Shaking of the Foundations*, a volume whose sermons have accompanied me since I was a boy listening to my father recite them from memory in our home. It is written in gratitude for Tillich's life, his questions, and the hard-earned faith that emerged from his own struggles.

Rather than attempting to recreate his theology, I've tried to dwell beside it—to sit at the edge of his words, asking my own. These poems arise from that space between certainty and surrender, from the stillness where human longing and divine grace recognize each other without needing to explain.

If these words offer shelter—if they give voice to something you've kept silent, or uncover a thread of mercy you hadn't yet named—then they have fulfilled their purpose.

This book is for all who dare to hope that grace is real, even now.

Especially now.

—*Ron Starbuck*

NOTES

1. Tillich, P. (1948). *The Shaking of the Foundations.* Charles Scribner's Sons.
   A collection of 23 sermons and meditations delivered between 1936 and 1948, exploring the theological and existential crises of the modern world. In these sermons, Tillich speaks of grace, estrangement, courage, and the unshakable ground of being, addressing the spiritual hunger of a world in turmoil with prophetic insight and pastoral depth.

2. Tillich, P. (1948). "You Are Accepted," in *The Shaking of the Foundations*, pp. 162–163. Charles Scribner's Sons.
   Tillich's defining meditation on grace and estrangement, concluding with the iconic phrase, "You are accepted."

3. Eliot, T. S. (1943). *Four Quartets.* Harcourt, Brace and Company.
   The title "At the Still Point" echoes a key image from Eliot's "Burnt Norton," a meditation on stillness, time, and eternity.

4. Scripture quotations are from the *New Revised Standard Version, Anglicised Edition (NRSVA)*, unless otherwise noted.

5. Miller, A. (1964). *After the fall: A play in two acts.* Viking Press.

ABOUT THE AUTHOR

RON STARBUCK is the Publisher, CEO, and Executive Editor of Saint Julian Press. He is a poet, writer, Episcopalian, and the author of *five rich collections of poetry: There Is Something About Being An Episcopalian, When Angels Are Born, Wheels Turning Inward, A Pilgrimage of Churches,* and *At The Still Point.* These works trace a poet's mythic and spiritual journey, easily traversing the paths of many contemplative traditions. For many years, he has been deeply involved in interfaith Buddhist-Christian dialogue, maintaining a lifelong interest in literature, poetry, Christian mysticism, comparative literature, religion, theology, and various contemplative practices.

GARAMOND – Garamond
Monotype Corsiva
Lucida Calligraphy
PERPETUA TITLING MT – PERPETUA TITLING